A MENTAL GUIDE TO TENNIS:

8 Mental Strategies to Up
Your Mental Toughness

TABLE OF CONTENTS

PREFACE

My name is Thomas Singleton. I am a Certified Mental Performance Consultant through the Association of Applied Sport Psychology, an avid tennis player, and a tennis instructor. I've had the opportunity to instruct players of all ages and skill levels, and I have two years of experience coaching the mental game of tennis to college and high school players. I've written this book to expand the scope of my mental coaching and to continue to help tennis players improve and play at their best.

I've also founded Perform With Presence, a mental coaching business, to advance those aims. To stay updated with PwP and our mental coaching efforts, please follow:

Our Instagram:
https://www.instagram.com/performwithpresence/

@PERFORMWITHPRESENCE

Our Website: https://performwithpresence.com/

Without further ado, let's get into it!

INTRODUCTION

This book will give you 8 mental strategies to use when you play tennis. It is my goal that this book empowers you to play your best tennis and to improve your game.

Before we dive into the 8 strategies, it's important for us to be on the same page about what the mental game is, what a mental strategy is, and how this book can help you improve your tennis and play your best.

The Mental Game

The mental game refers to how you use your mind in order to play tennis and improve your tennis skills. While the physical game of tennis takes place on the court, the mental game takes place in your mind.

Mental Strategies

A **mental strategy** is a tool that helps you use your mind more effectively.

A simple example of a mental strategy is focus. If a tennis player focuses on what they need to focus on in order to play at their best, they put themself in the best position to win.

This might mean they choose to focus on watching the ball extra closely or on playing to their strengths and attacking their opponents' weaknesses. In this way, focus is a type of mental strategy.

On the flipside, when a tennis player loses focus, or gets distracted, that decreases their chance of playing at their best. Distractions in tennis include anything that takes your focus off of the present moment.

I encourage you to think of mental strategies as being tools in a toolbox. Just like a mechanic relies on a toolbox to fix cars, mental strategies are the tools of your mind.

You want to be able to reach into your mental toolbox both on and off the court in order to play your best and improve your game.

At the very least, I hope this book adds at least one mental tool to your own mental toolbox.

I will present and describe 8 mental strategies to you in this book. I've divided the book into 8 chapters, with each chapter corresponding to 1 overarching mental strategy.

I've also divided the book into 4 parts. The first 2 parts cover mental strategies you can use off the court to improve your game. The final 2 parts describe mental strategies you can use on the court – while you play tennis – to improve and play your best.

Please note: All of the strategies discussed in this book are solely meant to help with tennis performance. They do not constitute mental health advice. If you are needing mental health support, please seek a licensed provider to receive proper treatment.

Finally, the strategies not marked with citations come from my own personal experience as a tennis coach, Mental Performance Consultant, and tennis player.

As you will see, I have cited research-backed strategies accordingly.

Let's dive in!

PART I:
GET A GRIP

As a tennis player, you put yourself at a big disadvantage if you don't play to your strengths. It's also crucial to intentionally practice your weaknesses. In Chapter 1, I will introduce a tool that you can use to play to your strengths and improve your weaknesses.

CHAPTER 1:

PERFORMANCE PROFILING

It is very important for tennis players to have a clear and accurate understanding of their skill set. The problem is, many players are not clear enough on their strengths and areas needing improvement. This makes it difficult to practice with enough intention to improve as quickly as possible.

Performance profiling is a tool you can use to become more aware of your strengths and weaknesses (Butler & Hardy, 1992). When you apply performance profiling to your game, you can use it to practice with more intention and to create effective game plans.

Before we learn performance profiling, let's look at an actual example of a performance profile.

Here is an example of a performance profile:

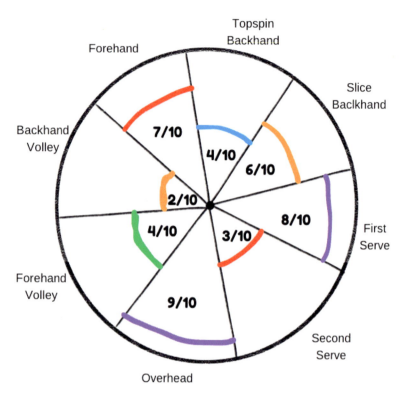

Forehand - currently 7/10. I need to add power and depth to make it 8/10.
Topspin Backhand - currently 4/10. I need to add consistency to make it 5/10.
Slice Backhand - currently 6/10. I need to add consistrncy to make it 7/10.
First Serve - currently 8/10. I need to add accuracy to make it 9/10.
Second Serve - currently 3/10. I need to add power to make it 4/10.
Overhead - my biggest strength at 9/10. I think I can add consistency to make it even better.
Forehand Volley - currently 4/10. I need to add power to make it 5/10.
Backhand Volley - my biggest weakness at 2/10. I need to add consistency to make it 3/10.

7

8

Here is how you can create your own performance profile:

1. Label the outside sections of a 'pie chart' with the most important shots and/or skills you use to play tennis. There are no wrong selections here. Pick the most important skills/shots that you use in *your* game. I recommend advanced players to identify more specific shots (e.g. backhand slice, forehand approach shot, second serve), while I recommend beginners to identify more general shots (e.g. backhand, forehand, serve).
2. Give yourself a rating that assesses your current ability level in each shot/skill. A general estimate is all that is needed. Color in or shade this section of your pie chart accordingly.
3. Ask yourself what you need to improve about each skill/shot in order to take it to the next level. Write your responses down next to your 'pie chart.'

Performance profiling requires you to 'look in the mirror' and self-reflect. Though it may sound corny, self-reflection is a powerful tool in tennis. It is a great way to use your mind to empower yourself to improve.

Here is why I endorse performance profiling:

Performance profiling empowers you to be more aware of your strengths and weaknesses. This knowledge enables you to do things:

1. It allows you to practice with more intention.
2. It allows you to play to your strengths in matches.

Let's dissect each of those benefits.

First, **practicing with intention** is key because, in my experience, lots of tennis players do not improve at the rate they could. **Practicing with intention** means picking 2 to 3 shots or skills to work on in every practice. Try this out for yourself.

Second, performance profiling gives you a roadmap for how you can leverage your strengths.

Say you excel at defense or keeping the ball consistently in. In that case, I would encourage you to avoid trying to win points too early and/or playing too aggressively. If you do this over and over again in a match, you will put yourself in the best position to win.

Conversely, if you know you excel at playing with power and offense and you lack consistency, make sure you take advantage of short or weak shots that your opponent hits. Look out for those opportunities every point.

PART II:
PRE-MATCH AND POST POST-MATCH ROUTINES

The best tennis players don't just work hard – they also work smart. Performing pre-match and post-match routines is a great way to work smart.

Pre-match routines put you in the best position to win before your match even starts, while post-match routines allow you to reflect on how to improve your game in real time.

I will discuss pre-match and post-match routines and their importance to your game in Part II. Before I do, I want to emphasize that you can and should use these routines not just before and after matches, but also before and after practices or hitting sessions.

CHAPTER 2:

THE PRE-MATCH ROUTINE

It is crucial for you to be both mentally and physically prepared before you play. But what does that really mean?

Physical preparation is somewhat obvious; your body needs to be ready to perform the movements necessary to facilitate optimal tennis performance.

Mental preparation is trickier. A lot of coaches and pundits throw around the phrase 'mental preparation' without actually defining it. So what does it take to be mentally prepared?

In my opinion, mental preparation requires three things:

First, you must have some kind of game plan or strategy planned for your match.

Second, you must visualize, or mentally rehearse, you performing your game plan before your match.

Third, you must be ready and willing to exert yourself both physically and mentally.

Let's briefly cover each element of mental preparation in detail.

Step 1: Have a game plan or strategy.

If you go into a tennis match without a game plan, you are putting yourself in a position where you are reactive to your opponent.

To put it bluntly, you are like a leaf in the wind; just like the wind blows a leaf in all sorts of directions and speeds, you are susceptible to however your opponent tries to beat you.

This is why I encourage tennis players to establish a game plan for each match they play. You want to give yourself every possible advantage you can heading into a match, and this step is key in doing so.

Even if you have no idea who your opponent is or what their strengths, weaknesses, and typical strategies are, you should have an idea of how you want to play to your strengths.

This is where your performance profile from Chapter 1 comes in.

Examples of game plans:

- If you know your backhand is more consistent and powerful than your forehand, plan to play it safe with your forehand and use the weak balls that your opponent hits to your backhand as opportunities to gain control over points.
- If you know your second serve is weak, plan to hit your first serve with a little less pace than possible in order to make more first serves in and avoid hitting your second serve.

If you do have an idea of your opponent's tendencies, even better! Form a plan that not only leverages your strengths but also takes advantage of your opponent's weaknesses.

Examples:

- Hitting your forehand to your opponent's weaker backhand side.
- Playing consistently and patiently and waiting for your overly aggressive or inconsistent opponent to miss.

Make sure you have a Plan B

As a final note for Step 1, I want to emphasize that you will often have to modify your game plan in the middle of matches. This happens when you and/or your opponent play in unexpected ways and is not uncommon. I call this a Plan B.

Thus, a game plan is not complete if you do not have a Plan B.

An example of a sufficient game plan is below:

- Be consistent from the backhand side and play aggressively when my opponent hits short/weak balls to my forehand.
- Try to find out which shot my opponent is weaker on - forehand or backhand. Plan to hit most balls to this side.
- Plan B: Be ready to adapt. If my opponent or if I start performing unexpectedly well or not-so-well at certain shots, adjust this game plan accordingly.

Step 2: Visualize

Visualization, also known as mental imagery or rehearsal, means using your imagination to practice your sport (Robin & Dominique, 2022).

Visualization is a powerful, research-backed tool you can use to improve your pre-match preparation.

Try it out! Before your next practice or match, close your eyes and rehearse executing each aspect of your Game Plan from Step 1 in your mind.

One way to make your visualization even more effective is do it with your racket in your hands and actually go through the motions of your game plans. I recommend players to envision and practice at least 3 different points from their upcoming match.

Step 3: Be ready and willing to exert yourself

It is important to remember that tennis can be very exhausting both physically and mentally. Remind yourself that you will likely have to work hard to achieve the outcome you want. Accept and don't fight the fact that often the most gritty, hardest-working player on the court wins.

CHAPTER 3:

THE POST-MATCH ROUTINE

In order to improve at tennis as quickly as possible, you need to have an accurate grasp on what parts of your game need improvement in real time.

As a post-match routine, I encourage tennis players to use a practical, simple method called the **Good-Better-How** method.

The Good-Better-How method is an activity that gets you to reflect on what you did well in your last match, what you could have done better, and how you can make those improvements the next time you play (Ort, 2018).

Here's how it works:

Good: List what you did well in your match.

Better: List what you could have done better.

How: Plan how you can practice those improvements in your next match or practice.

List at least one item for in the "Good" category and "Better" category. Make your entries as specific as you can:

For instance, don't just say 'Forehand'. For the "Good" category, ask yourself "What is it about my forehand that I did well?" Did you hit both your cross-court and down-the-line forehand well, or did you really just excel at one? What about it was good? Its power, consistency, and/or its accuracy? Be specific.

The same for goes for the "Better" category – don't just put "work on my shots in practice." It would be more helpful for you to pinpoint specific shots/skills you could have done better at. Examples include: brushing the ball more on my groundstrokes, watching the ball more closely, moving my feet so that I don't get too close to the ball.

For the "How" category, identify at least 2 actions you can take in your next practice or match in order to make the improvements you listed in the "Better" category.

Here is an example of a sufficient Good-Better-How reflection:

Good: forehand power, playing attacking tennis and moving forward, returns were consistent

Better: getting more second serves in, backhand consistency

How: focus on getting my second serve toss more in front, focus on aiming my backhand in the middle of the court

A final note: It can be very helpful to record your Good-Better-How reflections in a journal or even a note on your phone.

I recommend players to have a running log that they are constantly adding to.

This way, they can identify any trends that are present in their game. They can add this data to their performance profile and use it to maximize their practices and play to their strengths.

Once again, try it out!

PART III:
THE PRE-POINT ROUTINE

Now we will dive into mental strategies that you can use while actually playing tennis. The first strategy I will discuss is the pre-point routine.

Using a pre-point routine between points is a powerful mental strategy in tennis. I am dedicating a whole Part of this book to the pre-point routine because of how important I believe it to be.

CHAPTER 4:

THE PRE-POINT ROUTINE

This is how tennis works:

A point is played.

There is a break in play before the next point.

A point is played.

There is a break in play before the next point.

Repeat.

Repeat.

Repeat.

A tennis match is a collection of individual points, each of which are separate from each other. Treat it as such.

Just because you lost — or won — the previous point does not mean the outcome of the next point will be the same.

Even if you lost the last point because your opponent ended a grueling rally with an overhead smash winner, the next point is **completely and utterly** separate from the previous point. The next point is also completely and utterly separate from the last point even if you won the last point with a beautifully-executed drop shot.

The point is, in order to put yourself in the best position to win, you need to have a strategy for 1) letting go of the last point and 2) re-focusing on the next point.

This is where the pre-point routine comes in.

The pre-point routine is a process you perform before every point you play.

The purpose of the pre-point routine is to remind yourself to prepare for the next point. After all, anything could happen in the next point.

The problem many players face is that it can be extremely difficult to be totally focused during every point they play. And I don't blame players for this!

Tennis can be an emotional, tiring game. Being totally focused on the next point within seconds of losing – or winning – a high-pressure point is not an easy thing to do.

Re-focusing is crucial however. A tennis match is made of many points, often hundreds of them. If you have a strategy that helps you re-focus before every one of those points, you give yourself an advantage.

So let's take a look at what goes into the pre-point routine.

I endorse a 5-step process:

The **first** step of the pre-point routine is to take a breath. This surprises many people, but players often constrict or limit their breathing during points. So take a second to breathe.

Second, I coach players to perform what I call an **action**.

An **action** is a quick thing you do soon after you take your breath. Your **action** can be anything; it can be touching the back fence with your racket, saying a particular cue word or phrase to yourself, playing with your strings, or even the simple act of consciously blinking.

You want your **action** to be memorable for you. I've coached athletes who have chosen the "toilet flush" as their action. They make a flushing motion with their hand to "flush" the previous point away. Try this one out if it resonates with you!

Third, I coach players to accept that the previous point is over and that the next point is a totally new point.

Fourth, I coach players to note anything important that's going on in the match. For instance, you could ask yourself: Are you hitting a lot of balls in the net? Is your opponent winning with a certain strategy? Do you need to make any adjustments? So on and so forth. This is also helpful to do between games and sets.

Finally, I coach players to make a small plan for the next point. Refer to the last step and even to the game plan you made in your pre-match routine. Ask yourself what you need to do in the next point to put yourself in the best position to win it.

Here are the 5 steps in order:

1. Breathe.
2. Perform an **action**. Be totally focused on it as you do it.
3. Accept that the previous point is over and that the next point is a totally new point.
4. Note anything important that happened during the last point.

5. Make a small plan for the next point.

Tennis can be a zen-like experience if you apply the pre-point routine to your game. I, personally, love engaging in the habitual, point-by-point routine of this process.

A final note: It is ok to forget to do your pre-point routine sometimes! Don't go too hard on yourself here.

Just remember, your goal should be to focus on the next point, not the previous one, as often as you are able to.

PART IV:
ADDITIONAL MENTAL STRATEGIES TO USE DURING PLAY

In Part IV, I will discuss 4 additional mental strategies you can use as you play.

Please note that I've placed this section directly after the chapter on Pre-Point Routines intentionally. This is because I encourage you to use each of the strategies I discuss in this Part within your pre-point routine as you see fit.

Once again, I encourage you to use these strategies during both practices and matches.

CHAPTER 5:

MANAGING NERVES AND EMOTIONS

It is extremely common for tennis players to feel nervous in high-pressure moments or close matches. There is nothing wrong with feeling those emotions. I repeat: there is nothing wrong with feeling nervous. It happens to every tennis player.

With that being true, nerves can often hinder your tennis performance. A lot of tennis players call this "tightness" or "feeling tight."

Tightness gets its name from tennis players describing how anxiety feels in their bodies; tennis players often report feeling tense in high pressure moments (Simmons, 2020). This results in players focusing too much on their technique, slowing down their swing speed, moving more rigidly, hesitating through contact, and so on.

Because nervousness and tightness are inevitable, your goal should not be to avoid them. In fact, trying to avoid nervousness often make athletes feel more nervous.

Instead, I coach tennis players to manage and work with their emotions so that they interfere with performance as little as possible.

I'll give you 3 strategies to help you manage your nerves:

The Physiological Sigh

The physiological sigh is a breathing method that relaxes your body. It does this by activating your parasympathetic nervous system, the system that's responsible for physically calming you down (Lomas, 2024). You perform the physiological sigh with 3 breaths:

1. Inhale deeply and for several seconds through your nose. Fill your lungs almost to capacity with this breath.
2. Immediately follow that inhale with a quick and short nasal inhale. Your lungs should feel full of air at this point.
3. Exhale with a long sigh through your mouth.

I encourage players to use this breathing method because it's quick and can be performed between points.

I also like this method because nervousness doesn't just affect us mentally; it can also affect us physically.

For example, when I get nervous or tight on the tennis court or even before a match, I notice my heartbeat and breathing speed up and intensify. I also get butterflies in my stomach sometimes.

While these feelings are completely normal, I like to address this type of physical nervousness with a physical strategy. This is why I endorse the physiological sigh.

By using the physiological sigh, I feel like I'm combatting my nerves not only in my mind but also in my body.

Expressing Your Emotion

Expressing your emotion is simply that. If you feel a buildup of nervousness or tightness in you, it can help to 'let it out' instead of bottling it up.

Think of a sponge that's filled with water. Just like you need to squeeze the sponge in order to get the water out, you sometimes just need to physically drain the nervousness out of your body.

Here are 3 common ways I've coached players to do this between points:

- Perform some vigorous practice swings.
- Shake your arms and hands. As you do this, imagine that you're shaking the tension out of you.
- Bounce up and down on your feet.
- Yell. Some coaches may not like this, but yelling can be another effective way to drain your body of tightness

Similar to the physiological sigh, I like these methods because they address the physical sensation of nervousness/tightness with a physical strategy.

My philosophy is that you cannot control the emotions that you feel. Tightness will come and go as it pleases. So, instead, try to work with it. Have some strategies to combat it once it arises.

Peripheral Vision Strategy

This strategy takes advantage of your panoramic or peripheral vision.

When we are stressed, we often get tunnel vision. When we are relaxed, we take in more of our environment with our peripheral vision. In other words, relaxation is correlated with greater use of peripheral vision (Graham et al., 2018; TELOS Tennis, 2022). Thus, I like to use a peripheral vision routine when I'm feeling tight or nervous in tennis matches.

Here is the method:

1. Look at an object straight in front of you (e.g. the back fence) and begin to focus on your breath.
2. Keep looking at the object in front of you, but focus your attention on what's in your peripheral vision. Specifically, using your peripheral vision, pay attention to the scene above and below the object you're looking at. E.g. Focus on the sky for a few moments then focus on the ground for a few moments.
3. Then, using your peripheral vision, focus on the scene to the right and left of the object you're looking at. E.g. Focus on the section of the fence to the right of the section you're looking at, then focus on the section of the fence to the left of the section you're looking at.
4. Continue this for a few seconds or as long as you want to/can without interrupting the match.

Because this strategy takes a bit longer than the physiological sigh, it might be difficult to use it between points. Using this strategy between games or sets is very do-able however.

CHAPTER 6:

EXTERNAL FOCUS

What do you do when you notice that you're making lots of unforced errors? Do you adjust your technique? Do you slow down your swing speed? Do you aim for the middle of the court?

Making unforced errors in tennis is inevitable. And sometimes, there might be days where you make a ton of them. Sometimes we might even 'choke' and make unforced errors in high-pressure moments. Thus, having a strategy to stop making unforced errors is key.

One common reason a player chokes or makes unforced errors is by focusing too much on their technique. In high-pressure moments and important points, it's tempting to focus extra hard on the technique you use to hit the ball. This type of focus is an example of internal focus.

Internal focus is when a tennis player focuses on their own body movements. The problem with internal focus is that it often leads to choking, and a lot of sport psychology research backs this up (Roberts, Jackson, & Grundy 2017). This is why it can be helpful to use external focus when playing tennis matches.

External focus is when a tennis player focuses on their environment or the outcome of their movement. Examples of external focus include focusing on brushing the back of the ball, watching the ball extra closely, focusing on hitting your target, or focusing on the shape of the shot that you intend to hit.

I coach tennis players to use internal focus in practice, specifically when they are learning a new skill or adjusting their technique. I coach players to use external focus in competition and in matches.

I would recommend you to do the same. Brainstorm scenarios when you want to use internal focus. Conversely, come up with some scenarios when you want to use external focus.

The final piece of advice I want to give in this chapter is to focus on the shape of the shot that you are trying to hit. This is a form of visualization that you can use while you play tennis.

Timothy Gallwey highlights this in his classic book, *The Inner Game of Tennis*. He discusses the power of

33

visualization, and how it brings out the best in tennis players (Gallwey, 1974). I highly recommend trying this out for yourself.

CHAPTER 7:

SHOOT FOR COURAGE, NOT CONFIDENCE

Tennis coaches and commentators throw around the word 'confidence' frequently.

They emphasize the importance of playing with confidence, that confident players beat un-confident players, and that the best tennis players always play with confidence. I believe this is a mistake. I think confidence is overrated.

I coach tennis players to forget about whether or not they feel confident, and to instead **focus on playing with courage**. In this chapter, I will discuss what this mindset shift can do for you. Let me first explain why confidence is overrated.

Confidence is a feeling. Sometimes you feel it, sometimes you don't. And in my experience both as a tennis player and coaching tennis players, you don't have complete control over how confident you feel. This is why I coach tennis players to avoid focusing on their confidence level and to avoid faking confidence as well.

Instead, I think it is way more powerful to focus on playing with courage.

Here's what that may look like:

Let's say you're trying to hit the ball deep in the court, between your opponent's service line and base line. Before you hit your next shot, picture how you want your shot to look in your mind. How high over the net is your shot? Where does your shot land? How fast is it flying? How loopy or spinny is it?

This type of external focus can be useful not only when learning or honing a new shot or skill. It can also be extremely helpful when playing a match.

While you may not always feel confident, you always have the option to play tennis with courage.

To me, playing with courage means 1) being willing to take smart risks and 2) being willing to problem-solve against a tricky opponent.

Let's dissect those 2 elements.

Taking Smart Risks:

Common ways to take smart risks include but are not limited to: accelerating your racket through contact, trying to move your opponent around, aiming deep in your opponent's court, and moving forward to net.

Problem-Solving Against a Tricky Opponent:

Sometimes you play an opponent who forces you outside of your comfort zone. In order to beat these players, you will often have to adjust your usual tactics or game plan to try to make them uncomfortable. Here's an example:

Many players I've coached dislike hitting high backhands. When they play an opponent who consistently hits high to their backhand, they have 2 choices. They can keep playing the same way, effectively asking for more high backhands, or they can choose to make an adjustment.

Examples of adjustments are changing the height of your shots, playing more aggressively, hitting backhands off the rise, running around backhands to hit forehands, or moving forward and taking high balls out of the air.

The point is, often you need to take on the mindset of a scientist in tennis! Be willing to experiment with different adjustments and find out which ones work best against your opponent.

A final note: I want to emphasize that playing with patience *can* be another way to play with courage. This is especially true for players who typically prefer to play an offensive, higher-risk game style.

In a singles tennis match, it is very often that the most consistent player wins. When playing against a consistent player, it can be tempting to try to shorten points by playing extra-aggressively or going for winners early on in the point.

This type of offensive play can be a valid strategy. However, sometimes it's tempting to do this because you lack belief in your ability to rally and win long points.

The thought of grinding it out against a consistent player can be daunting. But don't always take the easy way out! Be willing to grind! Keep making your opponent hit one more ball in.

Sometimes playing with patience can be the most courageous thing you can do.

CHAPTER 8:

DO NOT CREATE A NEGATIVE NARRATIVE

How do you respond when you're not playing well?

Think back to an actual match or practice in which you played poorly. Before you turn to the next page, answer this question for yourself:

How did you respond mentally?

How would you assess your response? Are you proud of how you responded? What could you have done better?

Many players struggle to stay focused if they play poorly, get off to a slow start in a match, find themselves in a losing position, or if one of their shots seems to be failing them.

As I've emphasized in past chapters, playing poorly happens to everyone. Playing poorly is simply inevitable sometimes.

Before you hit the court next, I recommend doing 2 things. **First**, accept that playing poorly sometimes is inevitable. It's a simple reality, so give yourself that grace. **Second**, make a commitment to avoid creating a negative narrative in your mind the next time you play poorly.

So what does that mean?

Players often respond to poor play by saying to themselves "Today just isn't my day," "My forehand is really off today," or "Why does my backhand always do this?".

I call this action creating a negative narrative because the player is choosing to label their game as subpar.

Let's re-think this choice.

When you are playing poorly, the problem is not that you are playing poorly. Once again, everyone, and I mean everyone – even the best tennis players of all time – performs poorly sometimes.

I believe every athlete should accept this fact of life. The problem is that when you are playing poorly and, in addition to that, you assign a narrative to your performance that describes your tennis as being bad, you make it even more difficult to flip the script and start performing well.

One solution you can use to overcome subpar performance is to take every point you play one by one. Another way to phrase this is to take every point as it comes, or to be present for every single point.

So I really have 3 final messages:

First, make the choice to believe that every point is a new point.

Second, practice this mindset. Rehearse it. The next time you hit the court, make it a point to employ this mindset. If you do play poorly, remember to avoid creating a negative narrative.

Third, lean on your pre-point routine. After all, the pre-point routine is crucial because it is something you do to help yourself take every single point one by one.

Some things are cliché for good reason…

It's not about how many times you fall; it's about how many times you get back up. In tennis, this is the mindset – and the philosophy – of a champion.

REFERENCES

1. Butler, R. J., & Hardy, L. (1992). The Performance Profile: Theory and Application. The Sport Psychologist, 6(3), 253–264. https://doi.org/10.1123/tsp.6.3.253

2. Robin, N., & Dominique, L. (2022). Mental Imagery and Tennis: A Review, Applied Recommendations and New Research Directions. Movement & Sport Sciences - Science & Motricité. https://doi.org/10.1051/sm/2022009

3. Wolken, D. (2022, November 3). Some tennis players turn to VR as "Game changer" when they're Off Court. USA Today. https://www.usatoday.com/story/sports/tennis/2022/11/03/tennis-virtual-reality-sense-arena-jack-sock-jennifer-brady/8249187001/

4. Ort, E. (2018, January 9). Good, Better, How: Feedback for Med Student Success. University of

Nevada, Las Vegas.
https://www.unlv.edu/news/article/good-better-how-feedback-med-student-success#:~:text=The%20Good%2C%20Better%2C%20How%20approach,receiver%20is%20built%20on%20trust.

5. Simmons, P. J. (2020, September 9). Grace Under Pressure: 10 Tips to Combat Tightness. The Road to 4.5 Tennis. https://www.roadto45tennis.com/grace-under-pressure/

6. Lomas, E. (2024, March 8). The Physiological Sigh: A 30-Second Breathing Exercise to Lower Stress . Oura. https://ouraring.com/blog/what-is-the-physiological-sigh-how-to-do-it/#:~:text=The%20double%20inhale%20of%20a,system%20by%20increasing%20vagal%20tone.

7. TELOS Tennis. (2022, July 27). A 10 Second Technique that Reduces Stress in the Moment. YouTube. https://www.youtube.com/watch?v=_EvpTegIQq4&ab_channel=TELOSTennis

8. Graham, V., Dovorany, K., Bruton, E., Richards, N., Garbus, J., & Garbus, C. (2018). The Effect of Relaxation Techniques and Visual Training on

Peripheral Vision in US Collegiate Soccer Players. Optometry & Visual Performance, 6(2).

9. Gallwey, T. (1974). The Inner Game of Tennis: The Classic Guide to the Mental Side of Peak Performance. Random House.

Made in United States
Troutdale, OR
10/31/2024

24303029R00031